illusion(?)

a

book

of

poetry

Printed in the United States of America.
Library of Congress Cataloging-in-Publication
Data.
Wilks, Michael
illusion(?)
Library of Congress Control Number: 2011944606

Cover Formatting: Mike Baugher
Cover Design: Evan Gruber
Photographer: Julie Carter
Photo Background Artist: Anne Wilks
Senior Editor: Nancy Newman
Interior Design: Jean Boles

Beckworth Publications and the Beckworth
Publications logo are trademarks of Beckworth
Publications.

BECKWORTH PUBLICATIONS

illusion(?)

ISBN: 978-0-9847952-0-8
LCCN: 2011944606

Beckworth Publications
3108 E 10th St
Trenton, Mo 64683
660-204-4088

BECKWORTH PUBLICATIONS

Ordering information: Quantity Sales. Special discounts are available on quantity purchases by corporations, associations, and others. For details, contact the "Special Sales Department at Beckworth Publications."

illusion(?)

by

Michael Wilks

Introduction

When Michael's thoughts flow from ink to paper, he explores pain and triumph from his own experiences. He will tell you that some understanding comes from writing, but not always. Life is never still. Lessons are never learned but being learned. In one moment of clarity, Michael formed the plan for this book and upon reviewing the completed work embarked on the pursuit of a lifelong dream. Seeing his words in print and sharing his private thoughts left him to wonder if anyone reading them would find meaning in life as he did.

i used
to be
lonely
in my solitude
but now
as you are sitting here
beside me
helping
me to write
these words
i feel your
warmness
that takes away
the cold
in my heart
your spokenless words
make my thoughts
find all the happiness
i have always
wanted
your companionship
enlightens
my darkened
spirit
you stand
to go
and i stop.

time was
when we
knew
each other
all too well
but we had
never met
we always looked
but did not find
and now
we know
each other
in our hearts
and our souls
we search
for some sort
of guidance
knowing
that time will be
the one thing
that brings
us along
our lifelong
journey
together –
you
are
my friend.

i turned
around and you were gone
you went
quietly
on purpose
i am sure
not to disturb
my mind
the silence
makes me
wonder
if you will
ever come back
then i check
my heart
and know
that you are with me
and will never leave
your
thoughts
are the only things
i want to know
i feel
your touch
as you close
my eyes
to sleep.

the question is
is it ok to have
a dishonest
pleasure
in life –
as you judge
my question
that is
what you have
become
but i
must only
be true
to my heart and soul
to guide me
for your moral
judgment
is
not the truth
of this
life.

you feed
my soul
you quench its thirst
it wants
not when you are around
you
take it places
it has never
been before
you
care for
it as you know how
you
make its true nature
a reality
in itself
only
you
have been able
to do these
things
then why
do I worry
my soul
it hurts
when you
are gone
make your journey short
and
ours lifelong.

i thought
i knew
    a lot about life
      but discovered
    i was blinded
by what
    others
      might think
    about me
    but that is
      a lie
    for if i did
    i would not
      be who i am
    that
    discovery happened
    a long
      time ago
    but it is always
good
    to rethink
      yourself.

if love
is living
    on the edge
  then i
accept it
    and
       embrace
    it
  for making
      me feel alive
  in the way
i approach
    each day
   the dreams
     that
    turn into reality
are some
    of the precious
       moments
      i have
   and you
  make all of this
      possible –
   a twinkle
    to
     smile.

take a walk
with me
let me
show you
a little
of who
i am
and the why
of how
i get like this
first i would not give
you away
or could i even
think
about it
is there
a last
it would seem
too dark
to go there
so
i will stay
here
with my beginning –
i miss
the sunshine.

second
        fiddle
    is my role
        in our band
        i tried
            to learn
        another instrument
    but i could not afford
            it
        my worth
        diminished
            as time passed
        i saved my heart
            for you
        but it just
                wasn't enough –
        is there
                another band
        for me
            i doubt it.

are my lights
too bright
or
is my soul
so black
that anything
that illuminates
me
only causes
these feelings
to come out
maybe a room
with no light
would brighten
my soul
i tried
that
it did not
work either
so where
is my light.

i am paying
    a price
    for being
        in love
    with you
    my material wealth
                means
        nothing
                in this situation
        only the things
    i own
        and can give
                    you
            are my worth as a person
    you charge
                me nothing
        i only
                want
                    to give you
        everything
                of me
            but can you handle
                    that
        for it might be
                too much
            to bear –
        speaking of another bare
                how
            about
                    it.

our hour glass
has only
a very few grains
of sand
left
if i turn it
over
we would have
a lot
of new time
to start
again.
but we have
too much
in us
to start again
so
i will
just tip
it on its side
and
we
can have
forever.

i sit alone
listening
    to conversations
of life
    of jesus
of some mundane
        items
    i wonder
      to myself
is your conversation
worth words
    or could
a gesture
    of actions
make you
a better person
maybe you do that
    as i listen
    and
    try
    to learn.

Michael Wilks

my escape
comes
easily
as i hide
from you
in my hideaway
i surround
myself
with sounds
that i cannot hear
or care to listen to
if i don't
my world
would not be
here
which even
scares
me more
but i am
not afraid.

to rekindle
what we have
only takes
a word or two
a thought
might make
us think
of each other's
well being
we know
this won't
go away as we continue
to find solace
with each other
even though
we desire
for our physical
presence
together.

you are
showing
your true color
by what
you say and do
for me
and
to me
your internal
beauty
makes this soul
of mine
have spirit
i hope
i am worthy
of all
that
you
give
me.

i shake
with anticipation
wondering
who you are
or
have you changed
i only
know
i have changed
with my reflections
and
self conversations
i find
i love you
more than yesterday
which i
still
don't understand
but don't mind
either.

if you
  are always
there
    for your friend
    and
    think that
this is a pure
      natural act
    that you
        do without
    hesitation
    then
      you must be
a true friend
      and
      you are mine.

with us
we seem
to know
all too well
that our lives
will contain
each other
as the day
goes by
and other thoughts
come
we find each other there
we make
love
to each other
as we know how
we hold each other
in our spirits
and
our minds
we tell and
feel
each other in anything
and everything
our trust
grows
as we continue
to become
one
but ourselves.

i grabbed
all my beautiful
words and thoughts
that were
in my mind
i tried
to throw them
into your body
i put
my hands
on your arms
and
rubbed
to make them
soak into your heart
and soul
but when
i looked
into your eyes
i knew
they were already there
so i will continue
with new emotions
to keep
your spirit full
and
never want.

our lives
       have branches
     that we start
          with a little
        of nothing
      as we grow
                through our experiences
    we expand
                just like fingers
         on a glove
       those fingers have fingers
     those get lost
                in life sometimes
       and then when
                the love of your life
          appears
      you become crazed
          with exponential
               expansion
        that floods
             all
                of your body
                 and mind –
     will i stop
            only when
          i die
             now that
           i have you.

my reflection
i saw
and i looked
again
my hair
had darkened
my face
showed few lines
there was no
distraught
features
that time had made
younger no
happier yes
and then
like the sunrise
in the eastern sky
i brightened
to the moment
i have you
to thank
for saving
my inner beauty
from disappearing –
no contradiction
for my inside
ensnares
my outside.

come here
i want
to talk
to you
are you my friend
i think so
so listen
my life
is full
it does not
waiver
but it does
slip in and out
of being
sane and insane
what does that
make me –
thinking of you
my heart aches
but
my emotions
intoxicates
my soul
as i think
of making love
to you
i grit my teeth and my face contorts
the pain and the BEAUTY
of loving you.

i love someone
who loves me
which seems simple enough
but
she cannot
come to me
she must do
what she must
my heart
breaks
and so does hers
we fight
to be together
we are
such good friends
so where
do we go:
we take our tears
we take our emotions
we take our love
we take our feelings
we take our hearts
we take our Souls
oh what we have
would scare you
but we
know no fear
only true love and passion
that makes us
us.

we are afforded
opportunities
that we can and cannot
make the best of
i seem
to have a propensity
to screw
these up –
and why –
would be me
there is something
that ticks away
at me
that you do not understand
nor i
so i will continue
to disappoint
but i will not
kill myself.

i have a moment
to reflect
of what
we have become
we are
to each other
very loving
and caring
our other lives
are sometimes
in turmoil
that is why
we find
ourselves
when we are together
at peace
the grip
you have
on my heart
does not stop it
from beating
it makes
me strong
to be a person
of feelings
and emotion
i only hope
i do that
for you.

i tried
    to find
  your scent
      on my pillow
   i looked
      for your
         impression
    in my bed
   i wanted something
       physical
          of you
    but i thought
     you left your heart
        and your love
    with me
     and now
    that is what
      i have
   to put
      into my soul
   that is more
      than
    i could ever
   hope for.

i just
 want
to lay
    next
      to you
  and watch you sleep
to touch
your hair
    gently
    not to wake you
  to try
    to get into your dreams
  and if
      i saw you
    smile
        i would only hope
  that in your mind
      you have me
  for that
      moment
    of rest.

illusion(?)

you have me
   i cannot
      escape
  your passion
you have put you
      into my thoughts
    constantly
your vision clouds
      my eyes
    i see you everywhere
   in my mind
   we are not complete
   which scares me
       to euphoria
    so why stop
     i cannot.

i look
for a way
to find freedom
not from operation
but only
from self thoughts
of confinement
within my mind
the limits
that they try
to put
on me
only enhances
with clarity
the truth
that i want
and desire
if i continue
maybe death
will not kill
me
only make
me free.

you make
my words worthless
for how
i feel
about you
it cannot be expressed
in words
there are none
that hold
what i have
for you
in my heart
my passion
has no words
continuing
our journey
in a world
that we create
for ourselves
to find
each other.

life's
twists and turns
makes everyone
stop and look
at where they are
and for some
why they are
our lives
have
more than
its fair share
but those things
make us
stronger and closer together –
we are becoming
something
that no one
will know
only we
will understand.

as my thoughts
　　　encompass
and become
　　　　silence
　　i go to
　my innermost
i try
　　　　to find
　　the parts
　　　　of my existence
　　that few
　　　　know
　　　or care to
　i find you there
trying
　　　　to make
　　my soul
　　　　　smile –
　　　i continue
　　　　　to find
　　　　your words and thoughts
　　that take me
　　　　further
　　　　　into myself
　　as i examine
　　　　my worth
　　you truly make me
　　　　a better person.

telling everything
i know
would concern
even my friends
knowing everything
i know
would only scare
others
that don't care
anyway
knowing
who i am
would help
you define
the difference
between sane and insane –
the sun always rises
in the east
and sets
in the west
except
when it is
at its darkest.

i cannot mask
who i am
but my actions
often depict
an idiot
that only
stumbles
along
blind to the truth
i try
to reveal
my true self
knowing
that the mirror
reflects
those images
that only
lie to your soul
and keeps
you wondering
who you are.

it came
  upon me
  it tied
up my thoughts
it bound
  my body
  i shake
        with anticipation
    am i close
          to death
      or
          living
    with a damaged
          heart
    as i continue
          to long
          for you
    to set me free –
  to be complete.

unconscionable
to think
of my life
without you
i don't think
too hard
about it
for the pain
wrenches
my body
the bond we have
is so strong
no matter what or who
we will persevere –
across the world
we hold
and
caress
each other's thoughts
and emotions
as gently
as we can.

i have
to take you
into my arms
and
make you feel
you are not in danger
from
anything or anyone
but as we look out
standing at the top
of the mountain
we are almost afraid
we will fall
and
nothing
will catch us
so we jump
and hold
each other
until
we hit the ground
exploding
into our dream
we wake
to find
we are
at the top
of the mountain.

my mission
    may not have
a definition
    as we know it
there are attributes
that i know
    one
    of those
is
    to help
my best friend
    find happiness
when she looks
    inside herself
that task
    is heartfelt
but daunting
i will continue
    to fulfill
that what
she asks me –
for i have
her
best interest.

i thought
   long and hard
  about us
and what you mean
         to me
   your inner beauty
 radiates my soul
         and illuminates
            my mind
   to see colors
         of the truth
         of life
      you are essential
         to my existence
         and my happiness
       which will never
            go away
    only appear
         as a vision
    again and again.

there is a darkness
that few
have ever known
or would want
        to know
    it travels
    into the depths
        of who i am
        and what
        comes
            to raise
        its ugly head
        is crushing
    i feel compelled
        to tell you
        i have
    a dim light
        that tries
        to eliminate
            this coldness
i make love
        to you
    in my mind
        and
    the blackness
    is replaced
        by a still life
    of myself.

i try
  to collect
my thoughts
        to let
    this pen
look inside myself
        every day
    those things
            which i cannot control
        makes my destiny
            at times
        hard to digest
    it seems
            my judgments
        may be my downfall
    but then again
            if you don't live
        your moments
    you won't have
            any
        to die with
    only what if's.

those tears
you thought
were only for your cheeks
found mine tonight
were they
the same
i really don't know
but they were for real,
were they for the same reason
which is not the
same – i only
know
this
my heart and your heart
beat
almost together
so as we sit
so much apart
i wonder
as we have
our life together
inside
each other's soul –
please allow me
the ability
to love
you forever –
i kissed
this page.

wondering
as we look
at our lives
we think
that we did so good
we gave
our family
all that we should have
did we do right
by our family
?
but myself
has to be considered
so why
did i forget
myself
my family
would have been
who they were
with me guiding
not dictating
most importantly
i should have
told me
save
a little
for myself.

a desperate man
looking
for direction
i go inside myself
and ask
no one else
the only way
to find what
is missing
in me
is to find
me –
my search
continues.

i tried
   to protect myself
   but i didn't
   our love
         overwhelmed me
      i sit
            now knowing
   that i should have known
                  better
         you were and are
            the best thing
         that ever happened
      to me
            in life
      when it comes
               to loving someone
         you will stay
               for a long time
         until i drink
               you away
         or
         until i drink
                  away
      and that
         is how
            it ends.

that roller coaster
i was on
stopped
i started
to get off
i looked around
i took a breath
but before i could stop
it bolted
off again
up and down
left and right
i can only hold
on
and then i realized
i love roller coasters
for you make
them exciting
or is it
you make
my life
alive.

having to be here
and
you are not
i thought
that it was just
the way it is
and then
i closed
my eyes
and held
you in my arms
i kissed
your lips
so gently
that you looked
at me
and said
i love you
i woke
to find you
gone
and me saying
i love you.

finding that part
of you
that you thought
was lost
can be
the one thing
in life
that makes
you contemplate
the worth
of yourself –
we are lucky
a few times
to climb
again that pretentious heap
that we
always thought
was too high
but
not
now.

an artist
        paints
    with colors
and has the creativity
            to make
        what you see
                as your taste allows
            beauty or not
        as you take
                your brush
            and start
                    to paint me
            do you mix the colors
        do you see only black and white
            do you stay to a pattern
    or
        do you just step back
            and
            throw them all
        in your mind
        i must be
                too many colors
            all mixed
                into a conglomeration
            of this thing
                    i call life.

i only thought
    for a moment
  that you had gone
    the disbelief
    made my thoughts
      so clouded
    that i had
      to shave my head
    to focus
   i did realize
     you are gone
    to return
      when time
    will let you
      sometimes i love time
    for what
     it gives me
   as you give
     me
      your time.

i continue
     to sip
i squint
     to the page
i glance
     to the place
where more sits
i smile
          with anticipation
     knowing my girlfriend
is only
          a few feet away
     as she asks
               me to dance
     i take her hand
and tip
          to kiss
     her lips –
she still loves me
          for who
     I am.

sometimes disgust
        becomes my friend
     though it is not
           a good person
        to hang out with
        we can communicate
     to the fullest
           we have so many traits
        in common –
     i am sorry
           i disgust you
        even though i try
     my lot
        is not
           to win
        only to
           hope that life
     has a train
           for me
        and a ticket
           for you.

you make me
who i should be
not what
i was
that which we do
for each other
we breathe life
into
each other
we make all aspects
of our surroundings
absorb our souls
our senses
are enhanced
by our presence.

that old music
    brings back
  those times
     that make
  your spirit alive
   and
  your feet start
     to believe
   you can still dance
  time does these things
  to your body and your mind
but doesn't it take your experiences
   to make you
     wise
   only some
      find that true
  for they made life
   to live not to die
  they expand
     a universe
   within
     themselves.

sometimes
my friend
struggles
to find herself
her heart
is so big
it gets in her way
her kindness
is heartfelt
by anyone
who truly knows her
she makes
you melt
and
you think
if i could be more
like that
what does she want
i truly
believe
only happiness
that sometimes escapes
her passionate soul
but my beautiful
you will find it
only because
you deserve it.

if money
        was who liked
    me the most
  i would know
            no true human
        warmth
            only the things
        that money
                can bring
    no love
        no touch
                no caress
    only
  a relationship that does not fulfill me
  a something
            of nothing
  with you and i
            we have all
        that money
                cannot buy
            we are a fortunate two
    to have this wealth –
            my thoughts
        are constant
                of you
        i crave to understand
                how can
            i ever
                be with you.

how nice
is that
game
you play
with everyone
you meet
they are not
your friends
they think
of you
only as what you are
the alarm clock
is set
i hope
for your sake
within minutes
it will go
off.

as i find
    myself
  again alone
i try
    not to think
  of all the alternatives
      that could culminate
            my nature
        to think
            of being
        on top
            of you
  i run away from that thought
      as reality
        spanks my butt
      and then there
          i am
          again
  spanking yours.

sometimes
i never know
who is sitting
here
inside me
mean nice
complacent
stupid
intelligent
i just guess
but i am lying
to you
for i know
who i am
not.

noises
that we hear
  can bring
a smile
  or
a tear
  as we filter
those words
      we understand
  what we want
      and
  what they are
love makes
    us block
      those that
    are unkind
and tricks
    us to believe
  we can become
  something special
          for someone –
  i look
    to hear
    that noise.

confused
at best
is where i am
i need guidance
to help me live
within my own limits
i crash out
as darkness descends
wondering why
these emotions
are dictating
my every thought
conclusions
are not
as easy
as reality
might trick
you into believing.

the animal
in me
often talks
to my self
not myself
it comes
into me
around you
my control
becomes hard
to handle
every animal
can look
to pounce
and
i will with you
but only
when the time
has become
the moment
that we
both want.

i awake
to find
that i was not
sleeping
at all
it was a revelation
of why life
does these things
to me
fate has
many ways
to go
you can choose
your path
from what
comes your way
the trick
lies
in not where you
end up
but the how
of what
took you there.

you touched
my heart
today
as you always do
by just
wanting
to be with me
sometimes
which is all the time
before you come
everything
starts to become
a little delusional
as my fantasies
take me
my heart
transforms its beating
to a tumultuous sound
that i can feel and hear
you physically
change me
as your love
has become
an intricate part
of who i am.

the cold
that surrounds
me has nothing
to do with anything
except what
is inside me
as i lay here
trying
to understand
a part
of life
that seems to evade
us
as we walk
through all the if's
i look
to my soul
to guide me
more than my mind
can see
why does this stop
me
to reach
for one more time
that which
seems i cannot have.

passion
　　has all to do
　　　with us
　　we have
　　　　become
　　　an entity
　　　that has
　　a definition
　　　　of only itself
　　　it clamors
　　　　to make us
　　　envisage a future
　　　　　no paradox
　　　only a conclusion
　　　　that enlightens
　　　　　　our spirits –
　　　as a fragile
　　　　　piece of glass
　　　i hold your
　　　　heart
　　　as you
　　　　　do mine.

again there
was nothing
i tried
to initiate
but only got
emasculated
i need something
i need
the warmth
of a women
i want
my skin
to feel hers
and she mine
my mind
helps me
pretend in moments
my body
stops this
to bring my reality
of being
only me.

your violence
in your face
shows me
something besides
me
dictates your thoughts
i only wonder
but do not want
to probe
the mystery
of your misery
i can
hope
that mask
is temporary
and
not permanent.

by popular request
i ask you
back
you have been
voted
number one
by me
to have me
for the rest
of your life
i guess
your response
won't be
i do
the soap opera
of life
contains too many series
that have
us viewing daily
but it is
still
the most popular
with me.

our conversation
contains
the most honest
assessments
of who we are
we don't
predestine emotions
or hide thoughts
but we do protect each other
in some ways
someday
we will bare all
i cannot imagine
a more honest relationship
that
has all the ingredients
of true friendship
and
love.

you are
my angel
i cannot keep
you out
of my body
you come
to me
at no particular time
but all the time
someday there
will come a time
when
i hope
to steal
you away
and keep you captive
with me
forever
but i know you will come
willingly
with no regrets
only optimism
for us.

life does not
　　　tell the truth
　　all the time
　　　you have
　　　　　to be lied to
　　　　so you can
　　understand
　　　　life
　　　as people tell you
　　　　　is
　　　　　not
　　　what is real
　　this becomes
　　　　　so hard
　　　　with friends and family
　　　but what you know
　　　　　is
　　　　　the being
　　　　　　of you
　　　　　and
　　　　　　not them.

your friend
got into you
and made your ire
to him
extreme
but you know
and could tell
it wasn't meant
for you at all
it was
just his
miserable self
that has a best friend
he loves
with all his heart –
we kiss best friends
but forgive
them
more.

we lay
  with each other
 and take
   our hands to gently
           touch each other's face
        finding all the imperfections
             that make
             that person
                  beautiful
         to the other
        we have
            so much love
         to give the other
             without hesitation
         as your image
             fades
     i try
         to find my path
     my heart knows the way
       my mind
    will be the light
        and
      my soul
    will hold
            the truth.

almost asleep
but always
thinking of you
makes my reality
go a little better
everyday
for you
are the nourishment
of my being
that helps
me grow
into a better
man
my wish would
reciprocate
that which i give you
and make
your person
fulfilled
with happiness.

as we live
  this life
we hold our family
    precious to our beings
      our friends
        are gifts
        that we open and rewrap
      wouldn't be nice
          if in our lifetime
      our best friend
            was also
        the person
            that you loved
        in the special way
    that people
      have for
            their mate
    a thought
        to ponder
    a little water
      for that flower
    that grows
        inside your soul.

our tired souls
they try to sleep
with that
warmth of another
(only here as if it was real)
we see
our colors
they fade in and out
as our bodies
feel nothing
our mind controls
no thoughts
as our brain
relaxes itself
from constant thinking
of contemplating
there are no noises
as you are not here
and as it came
it went.

a man looks
to live
a good life
that matters –
to help
those he can
but the manipulators
make these efforts
null
for those with kind hearts
a knowing man
sees the truth
and makes
the decisions that are right
a man
who only sees
what he wants
finds no happiness
within himself
but an empty void
that will be
with him forever.

my love
i kissed
her lips
put my mouth
to her ear
unbuttoned her top
took her breasts
into my hands
then kissed
and licked
each one
i continued to sensually
go further down
to arouse
the animal
in her
then.

my ventures
   as i go through
   my life
are often
      different
   from most
only because
      i am
   who i am
everyday
      there is
   and will be
   my trials
      to test
me as a man
      i find solace
   in my friendship
   with you
      that helps
   guide me.

your eyes
they glazed
their look
within them
i saw the love
you felt
for me
i looked
deep into your soul
to let
you know
i feel the same
i have
all of those feelings
for you
having the power
to not
be able to look into you
i never
want
to lose.

my friend
i cannot
will not
let down
she has ideals
important
to her being
i respect
those
only for her
do i give
all of me
and my abilities
to share
our hardships
as our journey
continues
and our conclusion
is only
a guess
a hope
a dream
as i take the light
from the day
and give it
to my friend.

sitting alone
no sounds
that distract
my thoughts
i talk
to my pen
it says
the things
that i contemplate
about life
i always
wanted
a woman
who had all the attributes
that you possess
my eyes
cloud
my hand
shares
the feelings
of being so fortunate
to have you
makes the understanding
of a person's worth
somewhat
understandable
within the realm
of this reality.

what will
   i leave behind
  if i believe
    i was a good person
   that could
only be a trick
    of me tricking me
if i believe
   i was kind and helped
  someone become
     a better person
   that could be
   me tricking me
  if i thought
    i did exist
   for a purpose
   that i somehow fulfilled
  that again could be
    me tricking me
what and who i leave behind
    is not
   the importance of my life
  it is
   the internal worth
    that i become
   not as i was yesterday
  but what
    i was today.

there is
a fine line
between pain and pleasure
my pain
comes
with what i cannot have
my pleasure is
its own being
its own life
it makes
me
a complete person
with love and happiness
to give
and receive
their hand and hand
friendship
worries
my heart
but captures
my soul.

i see
 a glimmer
 a ray
that contains
 my being
 its wealth
 has been stripped
 it barely
 can stand
 on its own
 i talk to death
 about life
 and for my fortune
 life answers
 my closeness
 is not
 in moments
 only a moment
 is
 all
 i ever
 ask.

everyday
  i look inward
to try
  to discover
    those qualities
of life
    all of us
  look for
        but seldom find
      our judgments
          are the ones
      that allow us
            to experience
        the risks
          we are afforded
        if we walk
    always the straight and narrow
        do we live
          or
        do we just exist –
    thinking not knowing
          can be
        a
          good thing.

your façade
is predicted
on the illusion
that if
you create
this perfect
environment
then the result
of your endeavors
will be the ultimate conclusions
of our existence
and then again
your life
crashes
without real love
and
i still
wait.

loving you
is an adventure
that complicates
my life
with joys
and turmoil that comes
to my heart
i ask
for it
and i got
it
do i want it
still
i have no choice
it won't go
away
it is not like that
to love you like
i do
is a gift
full
of life's mysteries.

the distant whistle
you know
as your train
sometimes
i ride
other times
i watch
i don't know
all there is
to know
about it –
where is it going
how long is it
who is on board
or
(of course)
when will it
stop
that part
has always
intrigued
me.

all that
   stuff
  pushes me
to that side
    of my world
   that only
      a few know
   is controlled
  by the sensitivity
    of my moments
   as i analyze
    and dissect
    these emotions
   you give
     me.

that is what you
think i am
did you speak
from experience
if that is the case
then your experience
belies
that fiber
of me
you don't really
know
who classifies
the poor souls
of life
with titles
i would only
want
your help
if you cannot
then who.

as we chase
  our dreams
and catch
    those few ideas and ideals
  that not many
        will get a glimpse
    of
and as we continue
        to grow
      together
    fruition becomes
        not our goal
      but our own journey
    and its enlightenments
        are
        our
        destiny.

what part
    of silence
  do you enjoy
    the most
  is it thinking
    of death
  or just
    the feeling
    of loneliness –
  i engage
    both
   with a smile.

we both thought
this would
last forever
we knew
that with
all the distractions
of our worlds
our love would endure
our moment
has stopped
we stand
and look out
to see
each other
alone
for the first time
in a long time
i know
i won't go far
and all you need to do
is say
you need me
i will be there
my pride
i have none
when it comes
to loving you.

you told
me from your heart
about your feelings
that included me
that tantalized me
    to start
 my process
        of never stopping
        to love you
    all over again
            to sit and look
        at your beautiful face
        i close
            my eyes
                to imagine,
        life affords
        a few
            what we have
        the advantage
        we make
                of this gift
                is our choosing.

so we are
married
(not to scare you)
we will make
ourselves
true within
our commitment
to make
the other person
as good
as we can
with all the love
we have to give
each other
the end result
will only exemplify
the true
nature
of living
and
loving.

my thumb
met
my finger
they rubbed
against each other
they pressed
tight
to push
all that was between
them away
as they parted
they knew
that they had
been as close
as anything could be
without being
the other one –
reminding me
of two people
i know.

Michael Wilks

some things
are hard
to describe
it might
be in the laugh
with the joy
you bring me
as i do you
the scruple
of all
those innuendos
the symbolism
the ideals
the mixture
of pleasure and pain
the complicated nature
of us
continues
to make our bond
stronger
in the moments
we share.

it has been
   a long time
  since my thoughts
    have been
      this pleasant
  since my body
    has rejuvenated
   itself
    to become
 alive enough
     to want
  a day
    full of what
   i am feeling
would it be
    right
  to blame
 you for these
    euphoric moments –
i hope
  you can accept
    that.

where we are now
is
a place
that makes
sense out of life
we are
in the same book
on the same page
with the same word
it may not happen
again
so we will enjoy
our moments
together
as
we share our love
for each other.

my pleasures
in my life
are inclined
to be trite
and not contain
the worth
that they should
but with you
i find all the beauty
that holds
my fibers together
so i can see
another sunrise
that is not the light
of the day
i have that with you
in all the hours
of the day
we are inside each other
and
this
is who we
know we are.

what can
    i give
  you that no man
has ever
    i give you
my entire being
    heart
        soul
            mind
      i will take
care
      of you forever
                until
      i respect you
          as a person
    who knows me
          as i know her
      i can only imagine
        what a beautiful life
      with you
            would be like
        our friendship supersedes
            the deep passion
          of love
        we have
            for one another.

all the physical
            pleasures
      that life
               gives us
      our senses
            absorb
      and our conscious being
            reflects
      to console
      our troubled souls
                  only means
            that mannerisms
         of others
               seems
            so superficial
      with conversations
                  that are mundane
         as we flash
         ourselves
                  into our moments
            to set
               ourselves free.

i knocked
on your door
i waited patiently
for the snow
to melt
it was a while
you saw me through
the door
finally it cracked
ever so slightly
we talked
through
the opening
our conversations
lasted
for all the nights and the days
we could steal
you opened
and let me in
with this relief
my soul
was being fulfilled
our friendship grew
and then abruptly
it closed
to a slight opening
it went this way
for a while
until you invited me
in again

someday when
    i come in
    i will sit down
    and pass
   my life
        to you.

what time
we have
we should spend
together
being apart
hurts
both of us
until our
actual existence
is put
into jeopardy
(would anyone understand our
passion for each other)
we stop
and look
to leap
will be hard
and tedious moments await
when we land
we will be standing
with our happiness
as we are
then inseparable.

slept
    so hard
   darkness
was in my mind
   when i awoke
a light
    became as bright
   as i have ever seen
    it was your image
  your beautiful
      face
  illuminating my thoughts
i find myself alive
   with visions
     and
       fantasies
   of us.

we find ourselves
    in a risk moment
again
    these things
happen
    because of who
we are
and what we
    are inventing
for ourselves
is all this
    worth it
we ask ourselves
we both know
    that we have
a bond
    of souls
that will
last eternal
    within our existence.

we all
  want the goodness
that has
      been said here
   to meet
        that best friend-lover
   who knows
  you and you them
         better than anyone else
      to trust
   that person with personal
                  secrets
       you yourself
  have never revealed
 i have
       this in you
    but
   i cannot
         have
         you
    for you are
         my illusion
  and your being
       has not
            been found –
 if you
      were real then:

Michael Wilks

illusion(?)